THE TRAIL OF TEARS

The Cherokee Journey From Home

BY MARLENE TARG BRILL

Spotlight on American History
The Millbrook Press, Inc. • Brookfield, Connecticut

Cover photograph: "The Trail of Tears" by Robert Lindneux,
courtesy of the Woolaroc Museum, Bartlesville, Okla.

Photographs courtesy of the Philbrook Museum of Art, Tulsa, Okla.: p. 6;
Woolaroc Museum, Bartlesville, Okla.: p. 9; Oklahoma Historical Society: pp. 13
(Lee Hawkins Collection, #19451.44), 24 (#20516.1.13), 30 (top, #20516.1.43),
52 (#6393); New York Public Library Picture Collection: pp. 15, 44; Library of
Congress, Rare Book Division: p. 19; National Anthropological Archives, Smith-
sonian Institution: p. 20 (#1063-h-1); William L. Clements Library, Ann Arbor,
Mich.: p. 29; American Antiquarian Society, Worcester, Mass.: p. 30 (bottom);
Tennessee Tourist Development: pp. 34, 47, 54; Museum of the Cherokee
Indian, Cherokee, N.C.: p. 36; People Weekly © 1994 Ed Lallo: p. 55.
Maps by Frank Senyk.

Library of Congress Cataloging-in-Publication Data
Brill, Marlene Targ.
The trail of tears : the Cherokee journey from home /
by Marlene Targ Brill.
p.   cm. — (Spotlight on American history)
Includes bibliographical references (p.   ) and index.
Summary: dramatizes the removal of the Cherokees to Indian territory in Oklahoma
and details events leading up to the loss of their traditional lands in the Southeast.
ISBN 1-56294-486-X (lib. bdg.)
1. Trail of Tears, 1838—Juvenile literature.   2. Cherokee Indians—History
—19th century—Juvenile literature.   3. Cherokee Indians—Relocation—
Juvenile literature.   I. Title.   II. Series.
E99.C5B75   1995   973'.04975—dc20   94-16988   CIP   AC

Published by The Millbrook Press, Inc.
2 Old New Milford Road, Brookfield, Connecticut 06804

Contents

Chapter One
The Deadly Journey
7

Chapter Two
The Principal People
12

Chapter Three
One Cherokee Nation
18

Chapter Four
Broken Promises
26

Chapter Five
Government in Exile
32

Chapter Six
The Last Fight
38

Chapter Seven
Removal Begins
43

Chapter Eight
The Place Where They Cried
51

Chronology   56

Further Reading   58

Bibliography   59

Index   62

The
Trail of Tears

"The Endless Trail," by Jerome Tiger.

THE DEADLY JOURNEY

Quatie slowly pulled herself into the wagon. She checked that her oldest daughter had bundled the younger children and remembered to pack the family's few remaining possessions. Quatie's weak body shuddered from a blast of cold wind. Still, the proud wife of the Cherokee chief John Ross wrapped a woolen blanket tighter around her shoulders and grabbed the reins.

Tears welled in Quatie's eyes at the thought of another day on the road. Every mile brought new hardships for the weary outcasts—more hunger, exhaustion, and sickness. Yet the greatest sorrow was traveling farther from the sweet-smelling pine trees and red Georgia earth that her people called home.

Quatie and the other Cherokees never truly understood how the United States government could take their land, businesses, and farms. Why were soldiers surprised that they refused to leave everything they knew for unknown land west of the Mississippi River called Indian Territory? How could Americans be so cruel when the Cherokee Nation wanted to live in peace?

Quatie forced back the tears as she had so many times since leaving the army camp at Rattlesnake Springs. She needed her strength. Each morning her body strained to pack and load supplies. She hardly had enough energy to continue by bumpy wagon for 8 to 12 miles (13 to 19 kilometers) a day.

At night she ate little with her family before dropping off to sleep on the frozen ground. The icy cold winter had hit earlier than expected. Quatie must have wondered if she'd ever reach Indian Territory.

The Ross family was in the last group of Cherokees to leave their homes in Georgia, Tennessee, and North Carolina. John Ross was in charge of resettling the remaining 16,000 eastern Cherokees who had refused to leave at first. He took over the sorry march westward after learning how badly the United States government had treated the first Cherokees who had been loaded onto wagons and barges and shipped west.

The army had dragged many Cherokees from their homes with only the clothes on their backs. People who once owned plantations, animals, slaves, and gristmills traveled without shoes or cooking pots.

President Martin Van Buren had promised supplies necessary to make the trip. But government contractors delivered rancid meat and grain filled with weevils. Merchants along the way robbed Cherokees by charging inflated prices. Farmers charged high tolls for merely crossing their land.

John Ross realized they had no choice but to leave. But he wanted Cherokees to control the march west. He divided the travelers into thirteen groups and assigned each a leader. Then he hired thirteen doctors and ordered blankets and enough food. Before each group started out, John Ross inspected the supply wagons.

John Ross, the chief who was forced to lead
the Cherokees on their journey from home.

Even with the best plans death was everywhere. Fever, pneumonia, and tuberculosis claimed four to five lives each day. The hardest hit were the old and the very young. Babies born along the way had little chance to survive. After a death, mournful families stopped only long enough to chip shallow graves from the frozen soil. Then they continued without a word.

Each unmarked grave that Quatie passed seemed to drain more life from her. John Ross noticed his wife's sad and frail body. She never complained, but John worried because Quatie rarely spoke since leaving Ross's Landing in Tennessee. At Paducah, Kentucky, he hired the riverboat *Victoria* to ease her trip. John settled Quatie and the children below the crowded deck and covered her slight frame with a single blanket.

The powerful steamer forged the icy Mississippi and Arkansas rivers. By Little Rock, Arkansas, a blizzard forced the boat to dock. The travelers waded ashore and camped along the freezing river. Sleet formed on the barren trees. Some Cherokees slept in uncovered wagons. Others lay on the snow-covered ground with only the foggy sky above for cover.

Quatie nestled close to her children for warmth. They waited impatiently for the weather to calm before continuing. One night Quatie heard the cries of a sick child whose body lay exposed to the open air. Without warmth, he would surely die by morning. Quatie gave the child her blanket and went to sleep in a thin layer of clothing.

The child recovered, but Quatie caught pneumonia. She survived a few more days before the illness overpowered her. John Ross and his five children buried Quatie in an unmarked grave much like the one she had dreaded. One hundred years later devoted followers placed a headstone over the grave that read:

QUATIE
Indian Wife of John Ross,
Chief of the Cherokee Tribe,
Died in Little Rock,
Arkansas, February 1, 1839

———

The grieving Ross family plodded west for more than a month. Ross's party was the last to arrive at Fort Smith in Indian Territory, later the state of Oklahoma. They found that every Cherokee family from the thirteen groups had suffered a loss of someone they loved.

About 16,500 Cherokees left the Southeast by wagon train and on flatboats. Some died before the trip started, and others never regained their health in the new land. More than 1,500 were known to be buried like Quatie along the way. So many people died that the Cherokees called their journey *Nuna da ut sun y,* "the place where they cried." Later, the chain of graves from Tennessee through Arkansas to Oklahoma became known as the Trail of Tears.

Chiefs before Ross had warned the Cherokees that destruction would come. They recalled the ancient Cherokee myth about the West, the land of the setting sun. The Cherokees believed that where earth and sky met in the West lay death, "the Darkening, or twilight Place."

Ross later wondered if the movement west marked the "twilight of the Cherokee." More than 4,000 people died, and 16,000 were unjustly moved from their homeland.

Although the Cherokees survived, the Nation never fully recovered again.

THE PRINCIPAL PEOPLE

The Cherokees were once a strong and independent nation. They roamed more than 44,000 square miles (about 104,000 square kilometers) of hunting ground in what became Tennessee and Georgia and parts of North Carolina, South Carolina, Alabama, Kentucky, Virginia, and West Virginia. The heart of the Cherokee homeland rested in the Great Smoky Mountains and along the Tennessee River.

Early Cherokees called themselves *Ani Yun Wiya*, meaning Real or Principal People. The name reflected their importance among the southeastern tribes. Through the years, outsiders began calling them Cherokees. Some say this name came from the Choctaw Indian word *Chillaki*, or "cave dweller," which described the way some Cherokees lived in mountain caves. The Cherokees, however, regarded themselves as the Principal (or most important) People of their land.

The Cherokees lived in about sixty villages each having between thirty and fifty homes. Several groups, or clans, joined together to create a village. A head person, or Principal Chief, and warriors represented the village at joint tribal meetings held at

Chota on the Little Tennessee River. Everyday Cherokee government, however, followed village rules.

Each village elected its own council to resolve local problems. Anyone could speak at council meetings, and men and women had equal power. After everyone spoke, council women and men carefully decided questions of war and peace.

To the Cherokees, war was a way to keep a balance among individuals, clans, and tribes. Warriors proved their manhood by fighting in battle. The importance of war originated with the blood law. According to custom, blood must be spilled for blood.

War followed an enemy's attack. Sometimes, Cherokees

A French lithograph from the late 1700s shows warriors from a southeastern tribe. Artists did not make a distinction between tribes at that time.

fought to recover invaded hunting grounds. Or one clan punished another for the death of a member. Young Cherokees became experts with bows and arrows, blow darts, and slingshots, all of which were used in battle.

During times of peace, men hunted deer for food and skins in the forested mountains. Women planted maize (corn), squash, and beans in the village garden. They picked berries and roots along the fertile river valleys. Villagers shared a deep respect for the land and how it was used.

The Cherokees believed that land had its own spirit. The earth and everything that sprang from it were alive. Every peak and valley and cave had a story. According to Native American tradition, land was never owned. Instead, the Cherokees held their land in common. Individuals owned only what grew from the land or what was built on it, such as their homes. They took only those animals and plants from the land that were needed to survive.

Villagers established few formal borders with neighboring tribes. As long as land was worked and inhabited, tribes usually respected one another's boundaries. For this reason, the Cherokees never understood how European settlers could want land that native people had occupied for ten thousand years.

The first Cherokee contact with whites came in 1540. Hernando de Soto, a Spanish explorer, and his soldiers passed through Cherokee territory in search of gold. With them were about two hundred African and Indian slaves from earlier conquests along their route from the Gulf Coast.

The Cherokees neither feared nor admired the outsiders. They fed the steel-armed men dressed in tattered velvet clothes. Since de Soto's men found no precious metals, they moved on without a fight. The Cherokees took little notice.

Hernando de Soto approaches a group of warriors. Within one hundred years of the first meeting between Cherokees and Europeans, the Cherokee way of life had begun to change.

Few whites ventured into Cherokee country for the next hundred years. Occasionally, Spanish miners traveled from Florida to dig gold from riverbeds on eastern Cherokee lands. The Cherokees kept their distance and continued growing crops and hunting as they had for centuries.

During the 1600s, British colonists began trickling onto eastern shores. These intruders were different. They cleared the land and built towns rather than pass through in search of gold or slaves. When the British had settled one area, they moved farther west to claim another. French explorers paddled up the Mississippi River from the Southwest in search of deerskins. The Spanish moved closer to the Cherokees' southeast border. Soon each country clamored for more land. They never considered that the Cherokees had claimed the territory first.

These early settlers introduced the Cherokees to strange new practices. They brought horses, which Cherokee hunters rode to trap animals faster and farther away from their villages. Europeans also taught the Cherokees to shoot guns. Now hunters could kill many more animals than with bows and arrows. Guns and metal hatchets supplied warriors with far more deadly weapons to use against their enemies.

British and French traders wanted as many animal skins as the Cherokees could provide. They traveled into Cherokee villages to exchange cloth, metal pots and cooking utensils, guns, and rum for furs. Some white traders married Cherokee women and stayed.

These changes threatened the Cherokee way of life. Whites intruded deeper into Indian territory. Minor clashes broke out between Cherokees and whites. Southeastern Indian tribes competed for the fur trade to supply their families with everyday European goods they had come to depend upon. Tribes fought over hunting grounds they had shared in peace for centuries. Meanwhile, the fur supply dwindled, and land grew more scarce.

The Cherokees disagreed about how to treat the strangers. Most chiefs believed that if the Cherokees learned to live with the whites, then the whites would honor Indian homelands. One such leader, Chief Attacullaculla, sailed with six other Cherokees to London in 1730 to meet with King George II. The two men signed a pact that committed the Cherokees to support Great Britain against its enemies and to trade only with the Crown. In exchange, King George offered friendship and protection "for as long as the mountains and rivers last, and the sun shines."

In the end, Great Britain did little to keep intruders, British or otherwise, out of Cherokee land. This treaty was only one of thirty that whites refused to uphold before the final Cherokee removal from the Southeast.

A few Cherokee chiefs never trusted the whites. "Now mark what our forefathers told us," they warned. "Your elder brother [whites] will settle around you—he will encroach upon your lands. . . . When you give him a part of your country, he will not be satisfied, but ask for more. . . . He will point you to the west, but you will find no resting place there."

ONE CHEROKEE NATION

War broke out between the French and the British over land and trade routes in 1754. Cherokee and other tribes were drawn into the struggle for the control of riches in the New World. As always, the Cherokees honored their treaty with Great Britain.

The Cherokees soon found that British colonists rarely made a distinction between Indians who were enemies and those who were on their side. Two years into the war a band of Cherokees stole some horses as they passed through Virginia on their way home from fighting the French. Settlers attacked the party and killed and scalped twenty-four Cherokees. Although they were not completely innocent of wrongdoing, the Cherokees were convinced that the real enemy was the settlers.

The Cherokee warriors struck back in rage. They scalped Virginian colonists and burned their fields and cabins. Large armies of settlers countered by invading Cherokee land. Border wars lasted for another two years. By then, more than a dozen Cherokee towns were destroyed. Homes, granaries, and crops lay in ruin. Hundreds of men, women, and children were massacred.

THE AMERICAN MAGAZINE,

PRÆVALEBIT ÆQUIOR.

AND

MONTHLY CHRONICLE for the BRITISH Colonies.

This 1758 cover of The American Magazine and Monthly Chronicle *shows an Englishman with a Bible and a bolt of cloth and an elegantly dressed Frenchman with a purse and a tomahawk. They are each seeking the loyalty of the Cherokee who stands between them.*

An engraving of three Cherokee warriors and an interpreter on their way to London in 1762. The Cherokees got nothing in return for their loyalty to the British during the French and Indian War.

The French surrendered to the British in 1762. In the Treaty of Paris, signed the following year, the French lost all claim to land east of the Mississippi River. The French loss opened the frontier to new settlement by the British. One drawback, however, was the Cherokees.

The British began to chip away portions of Cherokee land. Three treaties signed between 1768 and 1775 gave the British most of Tennessee, hunting grounds in Kentucky, and land north of Georgia and east of the Blue Ridge Mountains. In return, the Cherokees received small amounts of money and goods and more promises of peace.

Cherokee Principal Chief Old Tassel said sarcastically, "If we had no lands, we should have fewer enemies."

THE CHEROKEES hardly fared better during the American Revolution of 1776. When colonists revolted against British control, peaceful Cherokees remained neutral. However, one young Cherokee chief named Dragging Canoe, who opposed any treaties with settlers, used the war as a way to regain lost Cherokee land. He and his warriors sided with the British. Great Britain bought their loyalty with gifts of hatchets, rifles, and rewards for each rebel scalp.

Dragging Canoe's warriors fiercely attacked frontier towns along the North and South Carolina and Georgia borders. After each raid they retreated to the Chickamauga area of Georgia, which earned them the name Chickamaugans. Meanwhile, the British navy raided Charleston harbor dressed as Cherokees. The attack convinced colonists that all Cherokees were dangerous.

The governments of Virginia, Georgia, and the Carolinas quickly organized a joint attack to crush the Cherokees. Six thousand five hundred men stormed Cherokee villages from four directions at once. Rewards for each Cherokee scalp ensured that no man, woman, or child in their path escaped alive. Soldiers plundered orchards, trampled fields, and killed livestock. Within a year, more than fifty villages were destroyed and hundreds of Cherokees remained homeless.

Before the bloodbath ended, the newly formed American states forced Cherokee chiefs to sign away another 5 million acres (more than 2 million hectares) of land. Treaties permitted the building of roads through Cherokee country. For the first time whites could easily travel across Cherokee land to some of the oldest Cherokee towns.

Displaced Native families founded new towns along the Tennessee River. Some went to Arkansas. Overall, the Cherokees were reduced to less than ten thousand people and one quarter of their hunting ground. Now the heart of the Cherokee homeland rested 100 miles (160 kilometers) west of Chota near the borders of Creek and Chickasaw lands in northern Georgia.

Angry Cherokee, Creek, and Chickasaw chiefs joined Dragging Canoe. Chickamaugans continued to raid frontier cabins that sprang up overnight on their former homeland. They chased away government inspectors who came to measure the land. Warriors smashed their compasses, which the Cherokees called land stealers.

Chickamaugan attacks lasted until the close of the eighteenth century. Widespread disease and death from endless fighting reduced the number of warrior raids. When Dragging Canoe died at the age of sixty in March 1792, many old ways died with him.

By then, a new plan had emerged to deal with the Cherokees. In the 1791 Treaty of Holston, the United States took charge of Cherokee trade and protection of new Cherokee borders. Cherokees received $1,000 a year as payment for lands they had lost to settlers. Cherokee chiefs felt safer dealing with the federal government than with the leaders of each new state.

The treaty also promised that the United States would provide tools for helping the Cherokees to change their tribe of hunters into herders and farmers. President George Washington truly believed that "civilized" Native Americans, meaning those who lived like whites, would be treated equally. Many Cherokees had the same hopes.

Washington sent agents to encourage the Cherokees to divide their land into individual farms. Agents taught the men to plant seeds and to farm with hoes, horses, plows, and other tools. They gave spinning wheels, cards, and looms to Cherokee women. The Cherokees were eager to learn and even more eager for peace on their land.

*T*HE CHEROKEE way of life had changed greatly by the early 1800s. With fewer animals to hunt, most men now grew corn and cotton and raised cattle, hogs, and sheep. Instead of pottery making and basket weaving, women wove cotton into fabric. Then they sewed the cloth into clothing similar to what the whites wore. Many white agents and traders settled among the Cherokees. Before long, large numbers of Cherokee children had names such as McDonald, Ross, and Saunders.

The Cherokees prospered on their fertile land. Log cabins with chimneys often replaced mud huts. Within a short time, many farms expanded into large plantations equal to what whites owned. Wealthy Cherokees adopted the cruel practice of owning black slaves. A few kept as many as a hundred slaves to work their vast fields.

Education in the white man's language became important to Cherokee leaders. In 1801 the first missionaries established schools

SEQUOYAH
and the
Written Word

SEQUOYAH, a mixed blood who spoke only Cherokee, questioned why Cherokees had never created their own written language. He experimented for years with different ways to capture Cherokee speech on paper. In 1821, Sequoyah completed an alphabet of eighty-six characters. The alphabet proved unusually easy to learn. Young and old mastered the system within days. Teachers taught the alphabet in Cherokee schools. Within a year the entire tribe knew about Sequoyah's invention, and many Cherokees could read.

Sequoyah's alphabet proved so valuable that, in 1828, Elias Boudinot began a Cherokee and English newspaper called the *Cherokee Phoenix*. The pa-

Sequoyah, creator of the Cherokee alphabet.

per's name reflected the ancient legend of the Phoenix. As it faced death, the Phoenix threw itself into a fire. A miracle occurred when the Phoenix emerged from the ashes to live another five hundred years. The Cherokees were proud to see their language in print like the white man's. They, too, would rise from the fire of the whites.

on Cherokee soil, and soon one-room schoolhouses filled with Cherokee children were a common sight. A few wealthier Cherokees or those who were married to whites sent their children away to school with white children.

"Remember the whites are near us," cautioned one chief. "Unless you can speak their language and read and write as they do, they will be able to cheat you and trample your rights. Be diligent therefore in your studies."

Broad-minded leaders, such as John Ross and Major Ridge, reasoned that another way to protect their homeland was to reorganize the tribe under a central government modeled after the United States. They elected a Principal Chief and a National Council to meet each October at New Echota in Georgia, the new Cherokee capital. The Council created local courts and organized a police force called the Light Horse. For the first time trials replaced clan punishment and the ancient blood law.

In 1827 the Council combined these new laws into a constitution. Under Cherokee law, the tribe was now the Cherokee Nation, "one of the sovereign and independent nations of the earth." The newly created National Council favored cooperation with the United States government. Still, they emphasized that the Cherokees would "allow not one more foot of land" to leave the Nation. The constitution called for death to anyone who sold land or signed a treaty that gave up Cherokee homeland.

Little did the Council know that in 1802 the U.S. government had promised the state governor that it would end any Cherokee land claims in Georgia. It had further promised to move the Cherokees out of the state.

BROKEN PROMISES

*M*any *Native American* tribes adopted white ways. Settlers called the Cherokees, Choctaws, Creeks, Chickasaws, and Seminoles the "Five Civilized Tribes" because of their efforts to follow European customs. Gideon Blackburn, a missionary teacher, wrote: "Thus far the Cherokees advanced further I believe than any other Indians in America."

Despite these peaceful changes, however, many settlers still argued that Indians were unfit to own land. In the end, nothing the Cherokees did pleased land-hungry Americans.

Georgia's population increased at an alarming rate during the early nineteenth century. Each year settlers tried to bribe or trick Cherokees to give up more of their fertile valleys. Georgia leaders were outraged at the Cherokees' bold declaration of self-government and aided the thieves.

Then gold was discovered in Georgia mountains near the center of Cherokee territory. Demands grew louder to move the Cherokees from their land. Miners full of gold fever swept throughout the Cherokee Nation. Some found no gold. But they saw the rich countryside and comfortable farms, and wanted to stay. Many formed groups called Pony Clubs to torment the Cherokees into leaving. Armed bands of looters overran Cherokee land. They drove off livestock, set fires to pastures, and damaged homes.

Until 1828, the federal government upheld Cherokee rights to their land over Georgia protests. They did little, however, to protect the Nation from attack. The state of Georgia and the federal government locked in battle over how to handle the Cherokee problem. Both had agreed more than twenty years earlier that the Cherokees should leave. The question was how and where they would go.

In that same year, Andrew Jackson was elected president of the United States. Jackson was a noted war hero and Indian fighter. His fame came from the Creek War, when brave Cherokee warriors fought by his side. Chief Junaluska saved Jackson's life at the Battle of Horse Shoe Bend. Major Ridge and John Ross led warriors who helped Jackson's soldiers win the battle. Yet Jackson never looked upon Cherokees as equals with rights.

Instead, he supported the desire of state governors to rid their land of Indians. One of his first acts as president was to propose the Indian Removal Act to Congress. He urged lawmakers to up-root the Five Civilized Tribes from the Southeast and resettle them in Indian Territory west of the Mississippi. Cherokee relocation to the present-day state of Oklahoma would take many years. But Jackson's presidency doomed the fate of the Cherokee Nation.

"If I had known Jackson would drive us from our homes I would have killed him that day at the Horse Shoe," said the aging Chief Junaluska.

One problem with Jackson's plan was Principal Chief John Ross. Ross was a mixed-blood Cherokee who had been raised as a full blood. He spoke English well and was educated in the ways of both whites and Cherokees. Moreover, he was an honest man who earned his people's confidence and respect. Ross determined to keep the Nation united and on their homeland.

"They look upon him as a god," complained future Georgia governor George Gilmer.

The Cherokees followed the lead of Ross and his admired counselor, Major Ridge. Major Ridge was one of the first full-blood Cherokee hunters to adopt the customs of white people. The Cherokees saw him as a hero of past wars and leader of the future. For a long time he called himself "Major" with pride. His old friend Andrew Jackson had honored him with this title during the Creek War. Now he mistrusted Jackson's friendship and preferred to be called simply, The Ridge.

The Ridge was right to mistrust the new president. Jackson was committed to helping Georgia leaders gain the Cherokee land promised them earlier. "Build a fire under them," Jackson told Georgia congressmen. "When it gets hot enough, they'll move."

Eleven days after Jackson's speech to Congress about removal, Georgia passed an Indian Code. With this code, the state abolished any Cherokee claims to self-government, thereby making Cherokee laws worthless. Cherokee gold fields were seized, and Indians were banned from removing gold from Georgia soil.

To further cripple the Nation, Council meetings were outlawed within the state. Cherokees were barred from speaking in court against a white person. A special police force called the Georgia Guard enforced laws favoring the state. Georgia imposed controls over the Cherokees but refused them protection under Georgia law.

These laws brought a new flood of violence against the Cherokees. On one occasion two white men dined with a wealthy mixed-

This 1830 engraving pokes fun at Andrew Jackson's role in the removal of the eastern tribes from their lands. Jackson appears as a towering father figure surrounded by Indians, doll-like figures whose fate lies in his hands.

Major Ridge, a respected leader and advisor to John Ross. Ross and Ridge would soon split over the question of Cherokee removal.

The front page of the first edition of the Cherokee Phoenix, *edited by Elias Boudinot.*

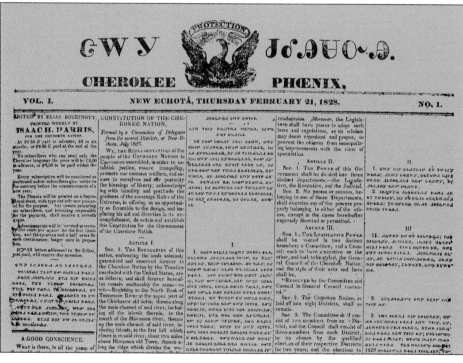

blood Cherokee. When the host left on an errand, the guests drove his children and their nurse from the home and robbed and burned the house. The men were caught and finally came to trial. However, the case was thrown out because Cherokees could no longer speak against whites in court.

Many young warriors wanted to battle the white land stealers. John Ross, The Ridge, and other leaders knew that open violence would give Jackson the excuse he wanted to overrun the Nation with soldiers. Elias Boudinot wrote in the *Cherokee Phoenix:* "It has been the desire of our enemies that the Cherokees may be urged to some desperate act. Thus far, this desire has never been realized, and we hope . . . this forbearance [patience] will continue."

John Ross and The Ridge appealed to the president to end the injustices. They traveled to Washington several times to argue for the land treaties granted them "for as long as the mountains and rivers last." They asked for protection against everyone who wanted their land—gold miners, settlers, and the state of Georgia.

Many celebrated whites supported Cherokee rights, but without success. "I am decidedly opposed to the Georgia claim," argued past president Thomas Jefferson. "She is the most greedy state in the Union."

With each protest on behalf of the Cherokees, Jackson held firm. He refused to guarantee the safety and authority of the Cherokee Nation. His supporters insisted that land granted the United States after the Revolutionary War included Cherokee territory. Each state governed the land within its boundaries, whether its occupants were white or Native American.

Finally, Jackson declared: "The President of the United States has no power to protect you against the laws of Georgia."

GOVERNMENT IN EXILE

Jackson further limited Cherokees by withholding payments to the Cherokee treasury that were awarded in the 1791 Treaty of Holston. The money currently funded projects, such as schools and the *Cherokee Phoenix*. Jackson redirected the money to start trouble within the Nation. His plan was to discredit John Ross and other mixed-blood leaders. Eventually, he hoped his agents could bribe enough chiefs to sign over Cherokee land.

Rumors spread about how mixed-blood plantation owners grew rich at the expense of full-blood Cherokees. A Philadelphia newspaper declared that the Cherokees were poor, wretched people who were ill-fed and in rags. They "traveled 50 to 60 miles over mountains to grist mills [of mixed-blood Cherokee leaders] to beg a peck of Indian meal."

Those who told the lies insisted there was only one cure for the problem—remove the entire Nation to the west. That way, they claimed, everyone could share the new land equally.

Georgia stepped up its battle to drive the Cherokees out. This time, the state enacted a lottery law. State inspectors divided Cherokee land into 160 acres (65 hectares) and gold mine sites into

40 acres (16 hectares). Lottery winners won free land with the spin of a wheel. The only losers in the game were the Cherokee families left without homes.

Soon Cherokee families found wagonloads of household goods outside their doors. Strangers flashed winning lottery tickets in their faces and demanded that the Cherokees leave. Some families were allowed to pack their belongings and leave peacefully, while others were forced out at gunpoint.

Sometimes homes and possessions were seized while families were away. On one return trip from Washington, a gun-toting stranger greeted John Ross. John rushed into the house to find his wife, Quatie, and their children gathered in two small rooms. The white man's family had taken over the rest of the house and seized the family-owned ferry at Ross's Landing, the livestock, and all the land. John Ross calmly packed whatever belongings he could and moved his family across the state line. They settled in a dirt-floor log cabin near the town of Red Clay in Tennessee.

OTHER HOMELESS Cherokees sought shelter in makeshift shacks or in the mountains. Those who agreed to farm 160 acres of land became U.S. citizens. They would do anything to stay in the land of their ancestors. A few believed they would be better off living away from whites and moved west.

In 1830, Congress passed Jackson's Indian Removal Bill. The bill finally gave the President what he wanted—authority to remove all Indians from the Southeast. Congress provided funds to buy tribal lands. Jackson approved several million dollars more to move the Five Civilized Tribes to Indian Territory west of the Mississippi River.

The log cabin near Red Clay, Tennessee, where John Ross and his family fled when a white man seized the Ross family home in Rossville, Georgia.

Jackson's bill sent shock waves through the Cherokee Nation. The National Council met illegally at Red Clay in Tennessee. Chief Whitepath, an older Cherokee leader, argued that Cherokees should reject the white settlers' ways and return to their earlier warring traditions. Younger chiefs wanted to move west.

John Ross knew that the Cherokees had advanced too far to turn back. His belief was that the state or national government would eventually realize that the Cherokees only wanted to live on their homeland in peace. The Principal Chief continued to urge nonviolence and unity.

Once again, the Cherokees appealed to Congress, the President, and the American people. The Council wrote: " . . . to remove [leave] from this land has no abiding place in our hearts. . . . We have a perfect and original right to remain without interruption or molestation." Once again, Jackson and Congress ignored Cherokee pleas.

The Cherokees had watched the removal of the other peaceful tribes. All but the warring Seminoles made treaties to move west. Each suffered from broken promises. The Council decided that the only hope for Cherokee justice was through the courts. They hired a white lawyer to plead their case.

The first of many rulings from the Supreme Court upheld Georgia's outrages against the Cherokees. The Court claimed that the Cherokee Nation was a "dependent nation." Therefore, the Cherokees must follow the laws of Georgia. John Ross refused to give up.

The main group to help the Cherokees oppose removal was the missionaries. They thought removal would hurt their progress in "civilizing" the Cherokees. The missionaries drafted strongly worded letters to newspapers and Congress that condemned Georgia's wrongdoing and opposed removal.

Georgia's response was to order all whites living with Cherokees to sign an oath to the state. Those who refused to sign faced beatings and jail. Whites who signed actually agreed that the state controlled the Cherokee people. The oath broke earlier treaties that allowed the Cherokees to govern themselves. Therefore, many missionaries refused to sign.

Samuel Worcester, a white missionary to the Cherokees who wrote for the *Cherokee Phoenix*, was one of those who resisted. Georgia Governor George R. Gilmer disliked Worcester's activities

Reverend Samuel Worcester, the missionary who was taken to court for his active support of the Cherokees. Although he was acquitted, Governor Gilmer would not release him from prison.

in support of the Cherokees. Still, Worcester was a local postmaster. The governor lacked the power to fire a federal worker. He also worried about critics who would protest his jailing a government agent. Jackson understood and ordered Worcester fired.

The Georgia Guard arrested Worcester and three other missionaries for staying on Cherokee soil without signing the oath. The Supreme Court had already ruled that Cherokees were without rights to trial under the law. Worcester, however, was a United

States citizen. White lawyers for the Cherokees brought a case before the Court on Worcester's behalf in 1832. They asserted that Worcester lived within an independent Cherokee Nation that was not subject to Georgia law.

This time, Worcester and the Cherokees won. The Court ruled that the law used by Georgia to imprison Worcester was unconstitutional. "The Cherokee Nation," wrote Chief Justice John Marshall, "is a distinct community, occupying its own territory . . . in which the laws of Georgia can have no right to enter but with the consent of the Cherokees."

The Cherokees were overjoyed. They celebrated with ancient tribal dances and feasts. Elias Boudinot wrote home from the North to his brother: "The question is forever settled as to who is right and who is wrong."

The Cherokee triumph turned out to be short-lived. Georgia Governor Gilmer prepared to fight the ruling and refused to release Worcester. President Jackson disliked John Marshall and his ruling and helped Georgia resist.

"John Marshall has made his decision, now let him enforce it," Jackson commented lightly. The missionaries stayed in jail, and Georgia continued to plunder the Cherokee Nation.

6

THE LAST FIGHT

One by one Cherokees lost their homes to spins of the lottery wheel. Government agents swept through the Nation to round up families to move west. Agents bribed Cherokees to put their names on lists for removal, and some threatened to kill those who refused to sign.

Agents convinced Cherokee Atalah Anosta to enroll when drunk against the wishes of his wife and children. When it was time to leave, Anosta hid. Soldiers of the Georgia Guard arrested his family and held them without food until his wife agreed to sign. Anosta reappeared to join her on a boat to Arkansas. At least two of their children died along the way. The saddened parents returned secretly on foot to their home east of the Mississippi River.

John Ridge, the college-educated son of The Ridge, wrote to John Ross that their people were "robbed and whipped by the whites almost every day." Yet, most Cherokees remained firm in their desire to stay on their homeland. Many believed like John Ross that they could outlive Andrew Jackson's presidency.

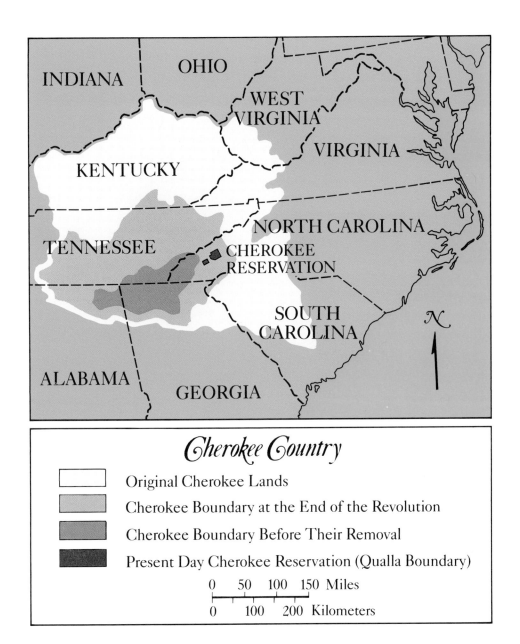

INDIANA

OHIO

WEST VIRGINIA

VIRGINIA

KENTUCKY

TENNESSEE

NORTH CAROLINA

CHEROKEE RESERVATION

SOUTH CAROLINA

N

ALABAMA

GEORGIA

Cherokee Country

Original Cherokee Lands

Cherokee Boundary at the End of the Revolution

Cherokee Boundary Before Their Removal

Present Day Cherokee Reservation (Qualla Boundary)

| 0 | 50 | 100 | 150 | Miles |

| 0 | 100 | 200 | Kilometers |

After the Worcester case, a small group of leaders began to discuss leaving. The Ridge, his son John, and nephew Elias Boudinot feared that the Georgia Guard would scatter all the Cherokees in time, wiping out the entire Cherokee Nation. The days of the Cherokee warrior were over, they agreed. The federal government was willing to pay Cherokees for their land and the expense of moving if they would leave now. Those who opposed removal for too long would be crushed and would leave with nothing.

At first, The Ridge and other leaders met in secret. Then they openly argued that the Nation would be better served if they arranged a treaty to move west. "We can't be a Nation here," John Ridge wrote to John Ross, "I hope we shall attempt to establish [ourselves] somewhere else."

John Ross pleaded for unity to keep the Nation strong. He stubbornly held that the people decided what he should do. "Our country and our people should always be our motto," he told John Ridge in a letter, "and their will should direct us in the path of duty."

Both sides agreed to present their case at the October Council meeting at Red Clay, Tennessee. John Ross opened the meeting by promising to back "the will of the majority for public good." John Ridge, representing what became known as the Treaty Party, requested that a committee be picked to negotiate a treaty in Washington.

The Cherokee chiefs rejected the Treaty Party plan. The Council chose another committee to go before Congress and appeal for relief from Georgia's unjust treatment. They selected John Ross to lead the group.

The Treaty Party was determined to have their own way. John Ridge, his father, and Boudinot agreed to leave Georgia. Moreover, John Ridge hungered to be Principal Chief. He decided that his small group knew what was best for the Cherokee Nation.

John Ridge and Elias Boudinot went to Washington to draft a treaty. Before leaving, however, John Ridge wrote the new Georgia governor, Wilson Lumpkin, about their plan. John requested that lottery winners wait until Treaty Party members went west before taking the Cherokees' homes.

Governor Lumpkin saw the Treaty Party as a sign that the Cherokee Nation was crumbling. He told his agents to "assure Boudinot, Ridge and their friends of state protection under any circumstances." Governor Lumpkin gave the Treaty Party $3,000 to pay for the trip to Washington. President Jackson slyly played one group against the other. He appeared to be neutral to both sides. But his only serious talks were with the Treaty Party.

John Ridge left Washington with the promise of $5 million in payment for land and goods left behind and to cover the expense of making the journey, building new schools, and starting a new life in the West. In return, the Cherokees were to leave all land east of the Mississippi. The Treaty Party also received guarantees that the new land in Indian Territory was theirs forever. John Ross's party left empty-handed.

News of the Treaty Party enraged the Cherokees. The party went against the Cherokee law not to sell native land. Some threatened to kill John Ridge, Boudinot, and others who drafted the treaty. John Ross opposed any violence within the Nation. Instead, he and other anti-treaty Cherokees banned the meeting called in the capital town of New Echota to explain the treaty.

On the cold, gray morning of December 21, 1835, three hundred Cherokees attended the meeting. The Ridge spoke gravely in Cherokee: "We obtained the land from the living God. The

Georgians got their title from the British. Yet they are strong and we are weak. . . . There is but one path of safety. . . . Give up these lands and go over beyond the Great Father of Waters."

On December 29, before Jackson's agents left the Nation, twenty Cherokees, including Treaty Party members, signed the Treaty of New Echota. "I have signed my death warrant," admitted The Ridge as he placed his mark on the paper.

Angry Cherokees rose up in protest. Nearly 16,000 signed a petition that declared the treaty a fake. Their supporters held rallies in many northern cities and condemned the treaty in Congress. Writer Ralph Waldo Emerson wrote to President Jackson: "Sir, does this government think that the people of the United States are become savage and mad?"

Jackson was unmoved. He prodded senators with the power of his presidency. Congress approved the treaty by one vote on May 23, 1836. Only a few Cherokees had signed. Yet the treaty required every Indian to move west within two years.

Most Cherokees remained sure that justice would win in the end. They refused to prepare for travel and planted crops as usual.

John Ross traveled to Washington many times over the next two years. He offered different plans for Cherokees to remain on some portion of their homeland. He pressed Congress to reverse the Treaty of New Echota. Ross hoped the new president, Martin Van Buren, would soften Jackson's hard stand against the Nation.

On March 27, 1838, Congress denied their final request for Cherokee relief. President Van Buren moved to enforce the treaty. Promises and threats had not worked. Only about 2,000 Cherokees relocated thus far. Van Buren ordered Major General Winfield Scott to remove the remaining 15,000 Cherokees. They must leave—by force if necessary.

REMOVAL BEGINS

Major Scott located his headquarters in New Echota. From the former Cherokee capital, he drafted a firm letter warning every Cherokee man, woman, and child "to join his brethren in the far West . . . before another moon passes." Scott further promised that his soldiers were "as kind hearted as brave."

In truth, the seven thousand soldiers swooped over the Nation causing the Cherokees to suffer greatly. Troops built stockade forts around the countryside to hold Cherokees awaiting removal. Scott ordered soldiers to use guns and swords if necessary to punish any Cherokee who tried to hide.

Soldiers snatched men from their fields. They pulled women from spinning wheels and children from their toys. Often soldiers crept up on families eating at the table or sleeping in bed. They forced the surprised Cherokees from their homes without time to take belongings or proper clothing.

Lawless mobs frequently followed the soldiers. Many Cherokees saw their homes looted or in flames as they were dragged away. Outlaws even dug into graves looking for silver jewelry and other valuables buried with the dead.

MAJOR GENERAL SCOTT, of the United States Army, sends to the Cherokee people, remaining in North Carolina, Georgia, Tennessee, and Alabama, this

ADDRESS.

Cherokees! The President of the United States has sent me, with a powerful army, to cause you, in obedience to the Treaty of 1835, to join that part of your people who are already established in prosperity, on the other side of the Mississippi. Unhappily, the two years which were allowed for the purpose, you have suffered to pass away without following, and without making any preparation to follow, and now, or by the time that this solemn *address* shall reach your distant settlements, the emigration must be commenced in haste, but, I hope, without disorder. I have no power, by granting a further delay, to correct the error that you have committed. The full moon of May is already on the wane, and before another shall have passed away, every Cherokee man, woman and child, in those States, must be in motion to join their brethren in the far West.

My Friends! This is no sudden determination on the part of the President, whom you and I must now obey. By the treaty, the emigration was to have been completed on, or or before, the 23rd of this month, and the President has constantly kept you warned, during the two years allowed, through all his officers and agents in this country, that the Treaty would be enforced.

I am come to carry out that determination. My troops already occupy many positions in the country that you are to abandon, and thousands, and thousands are approaching, from every quarter, to render resistance and escape alike hopeless. All those troops, regular and militia, are your friends. Receive them and confide in them as such. Obey them when they tell you that you can remain no longer in this country. Soldiers are as kind hearted as brave, and the desire of every one of us is to execute our painful duty in mercy. We are commanded by the President to act towards you in that spirit, and such is also the wish of the whole people of America.

Chiefs, head-men and warriors! Will you, then, by resistance, compel us to resort to arms? God forbid! Or will you, by flight, seek to hide yourselves in mountains and forests, and thus oblige us to hunt you down? Remember that, in pursuit, it may be impossible to avoid conflicts. The blood of the white man, or the blood of the red man, may be spilt, and if spilt, however accidentally, it may be impossible for the discreet and humane among you, or among us to prevent a general war and carnage. Think of this, my Cherokee brethren! I am an old warrior, and have been present at many a scene of slaughter; but spare me, I beseech you, the horror of witnessing the destruction of the Cherokees.

Do not, I invite you, even wait for the close approach of the troops; but make such preparations for emigration as you can, and hasten to this place, to Ross' Landing, or to Gunter's Landing, where you all will be received in kindness by officers selected for the purpose. You will find food for all, and clothing for the destitute, at either of those places, and thence at your ease and in comfort, be transported to your new homes according to the terms of the Treaty.

This is the address of a warrior to warriors. May his entreaties be kindly received, and may the God of both prosper the Americans and Cherokees, and preserve them long in peace and friendship with each other!

WINFIELD SCOTT.

Cherokee Agency,
May 10, 1838.

Hateful soldiers prodded and kicked the old and sick on their march to the camps. Those who were too weak to keep up were left by the road without food to recover or die. Soldiers pricked friends and family with bayonets to keep them from turning back to help.

As soldiers charged through villages, many children were separated from their frantic parents. One mother begged to find her scared children who had run into the woods. But soldiers steered her toward the stockade with the other prisoners, never to see her children again.

Boys and girls captured away from home were used to lure parents from hiding. Husbands and wives lost track of each other in the pushing and shoving. Anyone who tried to escape or run after a loved one was shot like an outlaw. One scared child who was deaf never heard the order to stop running and was killed.

A few hundred Cherokees outsmarted the soldiers. They hid in mountain caves and survived on roots and berries. One man, Tsali, became a symbol of hope whose story is told to this day.

Soldiers captured Tsali, his wife and brother, and his three sons and their families and led them toward a stockade. Tsali's tired wife paused along the road. The old man watched helplessly as soldiers jabbed his wife with the point of a bayonet. Later, Tsali told the others in Cherokee that their only hope was to take a chance and run away.

Cherokees overpowered the soldiers. As they fled, one soldier died and the others lay wounded. Major Scott knew he lacked the men to hunt Tsali and all the Cherokees hidden in mountain caves. Yet he worried that Tsali's freedom would set a bad example. Scott sent word to Tsali. If his family would give up, the rest of the runaways could remain free.

Tsali, his brother, and two older sons surrendered. A speedy trial found them guilty. They were to die by firing squad. Scott forced other Cherokees to shoot their doomed friends in an attempt to shame the Cherokees more.

Before he died, Tsali asked for one favor. He wanted his youngest son, Wasituna, to "die in the land of his birth."

As promised, Scott left Wasituna and the other runaways alone in the North Carolina mountains. An adopted Cherokee, Will Thomas, helped them buy about 56,000 acres (22,660 hectares) of land in the western part of the state. With time, this land became the Qualla Boundary, home to the Eastern Band of five thousand Cherokees.

John Ross returned from another failed Washington trip that summer to find the Cherokee Nation in ruins. Scott's soldiers had destroyed homes and crops and made ghost towns of the villages. By mid-June his troops had herded 15,000 heartsick Cherokees from Georgia, Tennessee, and North Carolina into overcrowded stockades like cattle.

The stockades were hotbeds of disease. Most were without roofs to shelter against the blistering sun. Cherokees usually ate fresh fruits and vegetables. Now their diet consisted of moldy corn cakes and bacon. The camps swarmed with dirty animals and lacked proper waste control. Hundreds of people died of food poisoning, fever, and other diseases.

The government provided a doctor for each stockade. But many doctors proved to be fakes. After a rash of sudden deaths, the Cherokees feared that the doctors were poisoning them and refused care.

Scott had begun the removal by land and water as planned. The first three groups of travelers each included about one thou-

Old Fort Marr, Tennessee, was part of a stockade where Cherokees were confined before they began their westward journey.

sand Cherokees. Reports soon reached John Ross that his people were in terrible trouble.

Guards crowded babies, grandparents, and sick adults onto dirty, unsafe riverboats. Several overcrowded boats threatened to sink. Soldiers unloaded the boats and carelessly picked those passengers who were to board again. They tore children from parents and husbands from wives. Some families were not reunited again until they reached Indian Territory.

Most Cherokees who went by land marched beside ill-equipped wagon trains for more than 800 miles (1,287 kilometers). Supplies rarely reached the groups on time. To make matters worse, the region had been suffering from a severe drought since May. Marchers wilted under the hot sun. Water levels of the Hiwassee, Tennessee, and Arkansas rivers fell so low that they became too dangerous for flatboats to navigate. Heat, exhaustion, and lack of water slowed the travelers. Of 875 Cherokees in one group only 602 reached Indian Territory alive.

Georgia Colonel Ziles wrote: "I fought through the Civil War, and I have seen men shot to pieces and slaughtered by the thousands, but the Cherokee removal was the cruelest work I ever knew."

John Ross called a meeting of the few National Council members left. The Council charged that Cherokees should oversee their own removal if they must leave. President Van Buren agreed to let John Ross handle the migration. He allotted about $60 in travel money for each Cherokee.

With the first payment, John Ross bought wagons, oxen, horses, blankets, soap, shoes, and mills to grind fresh grain into flour. Major Scott allowed Ross to wait until fall to leave. By then, it was hoped that the sick would be well and the drought over.

Late in September the rains came. Hundreds of Cherokees crowded into Rattlesnake Springs to prepare for removal. One large group, however, stayed apart from the others—about seven hundred Treaty Party members who had not left yet. These people refused to accept John Ross as their leader. Federal soldiers shipped their belongings ahead. Troops guided the Treaty Party members westward, including many who rode in their carriages attended by slaves.

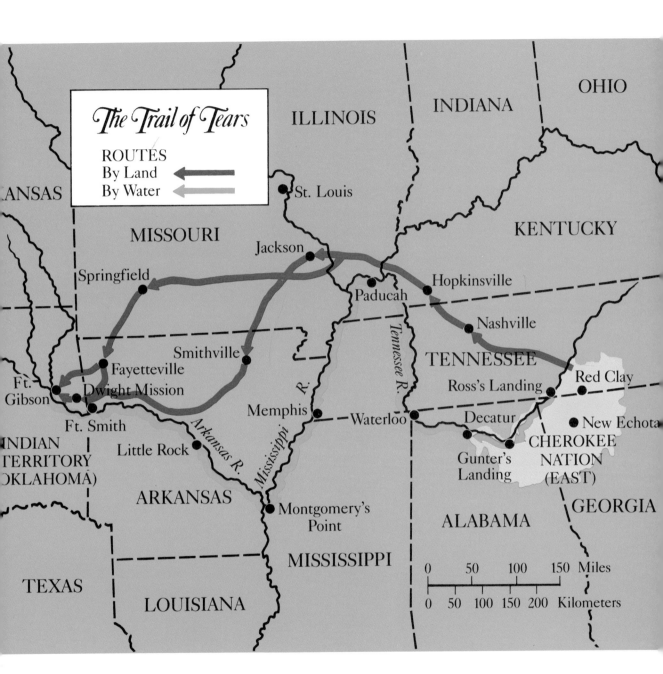

Meanwhile, the first of Ross's thirteen divisions assembled to leave from Rattlesnake Springs. A twisted train of wagons and horses stretched a quarter of a mile. Cherokee Light Horse guards waited for a sign to begin. The sun shown brightly. Children waved to friends who were going.

Most Cherokees looked thoughtful. Travelers gathered around sick friends and relatives who would stay behind. They shared words of encouragement that they hardly believed themselves. John Ross led the warriors in a final prayer. With tears in their eyes, the Cherokees took one last look at the mountains and valleys of their birth.

Then something strange happened. A clap of thunder roared from a single dark cloud in the western sky. John Ross's nephew William Coodey wrote that the giant drumbeat was "a voice of indignation for the wrong of my poor unhappy countrymen, driven by brutal force from all they loved and cherished in the land of their fathers." Other Cherokees worried that it was a warning about what was to come.

The thunder ended as abruptly as it began. The cloud disappeared in the noontime sun. As the bugle sounded, Chief Going Snake led the wagon train away—forever.

THE PLACE WHERE THEY CRIED

Every few days another division left Rattlesnake Springs. Each followed the same route up the Hiwassee River, northwest through Tennessee, and across southern Illinois. Weather decided the course from there. Some divisions continued west through Missouri by land. Others secured riverboats to sail down the Mississippi River and southwest along the Arkansas River.

Almost from the beginning, John Ross heard news of setbacks. Greedy whites heard that Cherokees had received money for the journey. Many falsely claimed debts owed them by the Cherokees. However, most Cherokees had no money. They had been forced to leave before the government paid them for their property. Heartless Georgians demanded horses, wagons, and cattle from unarmed Cherokees as payment.

George Hicks complained: "Our property has been stolen and robbed from us by white men. Why are they so bold? They know that we are in a defenseless situation, dependent on the Government for protection who they know have denied us that protection and Major Scott would not [help] in our behalf."

"Trail of Tears," by Elizabeth Janes, 1939.

Other divisions sent reports of spoiled meat and a shortage of clothing, shoes, and blankets. The weather worsened as divisions crept across the plains. Many Cherokees walked knee-deep in mud or trudged through blizzards.

One man passed the Cherokees "camped for the night by the road . . . under a severe fall of rain accompanied by heavy wind . . . and the cold wet ground for a resting place . . . even aged females, nearly ready to drop into the grave, were traveling with heavy burdens attached to the back."

John Ross prepared his family and 228 friends and relatives to leave with the last division. He packed the Nation's records and watched as the sick, aging, and children were loaded into wagons. Everybody else rode on horseback or walked. When everyone was ready, Ross drove his wife, Quatie, and the children from their home near Red Clay to meet the others at Cumberland Gap.

Ross's party reached Fort Smith in Indian Territory by March 1839, the last to arrive. Some groups had spent three months on the road. Others marched as long as six months through six states and territories.

Many Cherokees died like Quatie before crossing the Mississippi River. A full-blood Cherokee remembered: "Women cry and made sad wails. Children cry and many men cry, and all looked sad when friends die, but they say nothing and just put [their] heads down and keep on go[ing] towards [the] West. Many days pass and people die very much."

The death toll continued to climb after Cherokees reached Indian Territory. The strain from cold, hunger, and grief weakened the weary exiles. One in four Cherokees died because of the 1,000-mile (1,600-kilometer) march. Every Cherokee family had reason to weep from the Trail of Tears.

Cherokee misfortune lasted long after the Trail of Tears. Conflict developed between the first Cherokees who had settled in Indian Territory, Treaty Party members, and the newest immigrants. Six months after arrival, a band of immigrants executed The Ridge, John Ridge, and Elias Boudinot for signing the Treaty of New Echota.

In time, whites appeared on the new Cherokee land. First they trickled through. Then they came in droves and stayed, just like before. And just like before, the U.S. government did nothing to stop them. By 1907, Oklahoma became a state, and the Cherokee Nation under separate government vanished.

The Trail of Tears remains one of the greatest tragedies in American history. Cherokees, more than any other Native people, tried to live with the whites on their terms. Their reward was to lose their lives, homes, and much of their culture to the white men's hunger for more land.

Cherokee removal split the Nation forever into Eastern and Western bands. Many Cherokees survived to rebuild their lives in Oklahoma and the Qualla Boundary. Still, the Nation never rose to the same heights again. The Trail of Tears marked the "twilight of the Cherokee."

This eternal flame burns in Red Clay, Tennessee, in memory of those who died on the Trail of Tears.

TRAIL OF TEARS *Revisited*

MODERN CHEROKEES vowed never to forget this sad chapter in Cherokee history. To remember, more than one hundred men, women, and children reenacted the deadly one-thousand-mile march on its 150th anniversary.

The travelers set off in October 1988 from Red Clay Historical State Park, site of Cherokee council meetings from 1832 to 1838. They rode in thirty-two horse-drawn covered wagons or on mules. The wagon train climbed icy hills and battled miserable cold. But the adventurers continued until they reached what was once Indian Territory.

The journey lasted ten weeks but took travelers back 150 years to one of the greatest tragedies for the Cherokee Nation. In 1988 the U.S. government officially marked the Cherokees' route along the Trail of Tears as a National Historic Trail.

In November 1988 a wagon train set out to follow the route taken by nearly 15,000 Cherokees one hundred and fifty years before.

Chronology

1540   Spanish explorer Hernando de Soto is the first white to visit Cherokee country.

1600s   British, French, and Spanish traders and settlers trickle into Cherokee territory.

1754–1763   Cherokees fight with the British in the French and Indian War. The French surrender to the British all claim to land east of the Mississippi River, including Cherokee territory.

1768–1775   Three treaties are signed between the Cherokees and the British that rob the Cherokees of much of their territory in Tennessee, Kentucky, and northeast Georgia.

1802   Georgia and the U.S. government agree to end Cherokee land claims and move the tribe from the state.

1827   Cherokees draft a constitution that declares them an independent nation.

1828   Elias Boudinot publishes the first Cherokee-English newspaper, the *Cherokee Phoenix*.

1829   Georgia passes the Indian Code, abolishing all Cherokee rights and claims of independence.

1830	Congress passes the Indian Removal Bill.
1831	President Andrew Jackson cuts off government payments to the Cherokee Nation. The Supreme Court decides not to recognize the Cherokees as a separate nation.
1832	The Ridge, John Ridge, and Elias Boudinot form the Treaty Party to persuade other Cherokees to move west.
1835	Treaty Party members sign the Treaty of New Echota, selling all Cherokee land east of the Mississippi River to the U.S. government.
1838–1839	The Cherokee removal begins. Tsali surrenders to Major Scott so other Cherokees who fled into the mountains can stay in North Carolina, forming the Eastern Band of Cherokees. Four thousand Cherokees die on the journey to Indian Territory called the Trail of Tears.
1907	Oklahoma gains its statehood. The Cherokee Nation as a separate government ceases to exist.

Further Reading

Clark, Electa. Cherokee Chief: *The Life of John Ross*. New York: The Macmillan Company, 1970.

Fleishmann, Glen. *The Cherokee Removal*. New York: Franklin Watts, 1971.

Harrell, Sara Gordon. *John Ross: The Story of an American Indian*. Minneapolis, Minn.: Dillon Press, 1979.

Landau, Elaine. *The Cherokees*. New York: Franklin Watts, 1992.

Lucas, Eileen. *The Cherokees: People of the Southeast*. Brookfield, Conn.: The Millbrook Press, 1993.

Perdue, Theda. *The Cherokee*. New York: Chelsea House, 1989.

Petersen, David. *Sequoyah, Father of the Cherokee Alphabet*. Chicago: Childrens Press, 1991.

Stein, Conrad. *The Story of the Trail of Tears*. Chicago: Childrens Press, 1985.

Waldman, Carl. *Atlas of the North American Indian*. New York: Facts on File, 1985.

Waldman, Carl. *Encyclopedia of Native American Tribes*. New York: Facts on File, 1988.

Bibliography

The author wishes to thank the following Native American and national historical organizations for resource materials and assistance:

Cherokee Heritage Center
Box 515
Tahlequah, Oklahoma 74465
(918) 456-6195

Cherokee Visitors' Center
Box 465
Cherokee, North Carolina 28719
(800) 222-6157

New Echota State Park
New Echota Historic Site, 1211 Chatsworth Highway
Calhoun, Georgia 30701
(404) 629-8151.

Red Clay Historical Park
Route 6, Box 306
Cleveland, Tennessee 37311
(615) 478-0339

Sources for *The Trail of Tears* include reference books, histories, Native American biographies, periodicals, and reports of oral histories. Many original sources are located at the Native American Educational Service and Newberry Library in Chicago. The Newberry Library holds a vast amount of material in the Ayer Collection, including the John Howard Payne Papers, original *Cherokee Phoenix* newspapers, congressional records, and letters from the Bureau of Indian Affairs.

Carter, Samuel, III. *Cherokee Sunset: A Nation Betrayed*. Garden City, New York: Doubleday and Company, 1976.

Cherokee Phoenix. February 11, 1829, quoting the *Connecticut Journal;* February 25, 1829; March 3, 1830, quoting Thomas Jefferson and the *New York Observer;* May 10, 1838, Major General Winfield Scott's letter to the Cherokees.

Collier, Peter. *When Shall They Rest?* New York: Holt, Rinehart and Winston, 1973.

de Baillou, Clemens, ed. "John Howard Payne and His Countrymen." Athens, Georgia, 1961.

Eaton, Rachel. *John Ross and the Cherokee Indians*. Menacha, Wisconsin: Bantam Publishing, 1921.

Ellis, Jerry. *Walking the Trail*. New York: Delacorte Press, 1991.

Foreman, Grant, ed. Indian Justice: A Cherokee Murder Trial at Tahlequah in 1840 as Reported by John Howard Payne. Oklahoma City, 1934.

Jahoda, Gloria. *The Trail of Tears: The Story of the American Indian Removals, 1813–1855*. Papers on file at the Native American Educational Service, Chicago.

Kilpatrick, Jack, ed. *New Echota Letter: Contributions of Samuel A. Worcester of the Cherokee Phoenix*. Dallas: Southern Methodist University Press, 1968.

Maddox, Cynthia. "On the Cherokee Trail of Tears." *Southern Living*, September 1988.

Mails, Thomas. *The Cherokee People*. Tulsa, Oklahoma: Council Oak Books, 1992.

McLoughlin, William. *Cherokee Renascence in the Republic*. Princeton, New Jersey: Princeton University Press, 1986.

Mooney, James. *Myths of the Cherokee*. Washington: Bureau of American Ethnology, 19th Annual Report, Part 1, 1900.

Moulton, John, ed. *The Papers of Chief John Ross*. Vol. 1, 1807–1839. Norman, Oklahoma: University of Oklahoma Press, 1985.

Perdue, Theda. *The Cherokee*. New York: Chelsea House, 1989.

Shaw, Bill. "Paying Homage to a Brutalized People: A Wagon Train Follows the Infamous Trail of Tears." *People*, December 12, 1988.

Wilkins, Thurman. *Cherokee Tragedy*. New York: The Macmillan Company, 1970.

Index

Page numbers in *italics* refer
to illustrations.

Alabama, 12
Alphabet, Cherokee, 24
American Revolution, 21-22
Ani Yun Wiya, 12
Anosta, Atalah, 38
Arkansas, 11, 22
Arkansas River, 51
Attacullaculla, Chief, 17

Blackburn, Gideon, 26
Boudinot, Elias, 24, 30, 31, 37, 40,
    41, 53

Cherokee Indians
    alphabet of, 24
    American Revolution and, 21-22
    during Creek War, 27, 28

early contacts with whites, 14,
    16-17
education and, 23, 25
government of, 12-13, 25
land, view of, 14
removal policy and, 27, 28, 32-
    38, 40-43
Supreme Court rulings and, 35-37
Trail of Tears, 7-8, 10-11, 43, 45-
    48, 50-54
treaties with Britain, 17, 18, 21
war, importance of, 13-14
Washington and, 23
women, 13, 14
Cherokee Nation, formation of, 25
Cherokee Phoenix, 24, *30*, 31
Chickamaugan Indians, 21, 22
Chickasaw Indians, 22, 26
Choctaw Indians, 12, 26

Coodey, William, 50
Creek Indians, 22, 26
Creek War, 27, 28
Crops, 14

Disease, 10, 46
Dragging Canoe, Chief, 21, 22

Eastern Band, 46, 54
Education, 23, 25
Emerson, Ralph Waldo, 42
"Endless Trail, The" (Tiger), *6*

Five Civilized Tribes, 26, 27, 33
Fort Smith, 11, 53
France
   explorers, 16, *19*
   in French and Indian War, 18, 20
Fur trade, 16, 17

George II, king of England, 17
Georgia, 7, 8, 12, 21, 25-28, 31-33,
   35-38, 40-42
Georgia Guard, 28, 36, 40
Gilmer, George R., 28, 35-37
Going Snake, Chief, 50
Gold, 25, 28
Government, Cherokee, 12-13, 25
Great Britain
   colonists, 16, *19*
   in French and Indian War, 18, 20
   treaties with Cherokees, 17, 18,
   21
Great Smoky Mountains, 12

Hicks, George, 51
Hiwassee River, 51
Holston, Treaty of (1791), 22-23, 32
Horses, 16
Horse Shoe Bend, Battle of, 27

Illinois, 51
Indian Code, 28
Indian Removal Act (1830), 27, 33
Indian Territory, 7, 11, 27, 33, 41

Jackson, Andrew, 27, 28, *29*, 31-38,
   41, 42
Janes, Elizabeth, *52*
Jefferson, Thomas, 31
Junaluska, Chief, 27

Kentucky, 12, 21

Land, Cherokee view of, 14
Light Horse (police force), 25, 50
Lottery law, 32-33, 38
Lumpkin, William, 41

Marshall, John, 37
Missionaries, 23, 35, 36
Mississippi River, 51

National Council, 25, 34, 35, 40, 48
National Historic Trail, 55
New Echota, 25, 43
New Echota, Treaty of (1835), 42,
   53
North Carolina, 8, 12, 21, 46

Oklahoma, 11, 54
Old Fort Marr, *47*
Old Tassel, Chief, 21

Paris, Treaty of (1763), 20
Phoenix, legend of, 24

Qualla Boundary, 46, 54

Rattlesnake Springs, 7, 48, 50
Red Clay, Tennessee, 33, 34, *34,
    54*, 55
Ridge, John, 38, 40-41, 53
Ridge, The (Major), 25, 27, 28, *30,*
    31, 40-42, 53
Ross, John, 7, 8, *9,* 10-11, 25, 27-
    28, 31-35, 38, 40-42, 46-48, 50,
    51, 53
Ross, Quatie, 7-8, 10-11, 33, 53

Scott, Winfield, 42, 43, 45-46, 48,
    51
Seminole Indians, 26, 35
Sequoyah, 24, *24*
Slavery, 23
Soto, Hernando de, 14, *15*
South Carolina, 12, 21
Spanish explorers, 14, 16

Supreme Court of the United
    States, 35-37

Tennessee, 8, 11, 12, 21, 33, 34,
    34, 51, *54*
Tennessee River, 12, 22
Thomas, Will, 46
Tiger, Jerome, *6*
Trail of Tears, 7-8, 10-11, 43, 45-
    48, 50-54
"Trail of Tears" (Janes), *52*
Treaty Party, 40-41, 48, 53
Tsali, 45-46

Van Buren, Martin, 8, 42, 48
Villages, 12-13
Virginia, 12, 18, 21

War, importance of, 13-14
Washington, George, 23
Wasituna, 46
Western Band, 54
West Virginia, 12
Whitepath, Chief, 34
Women, 13, 14
Worcester, Samuel, 35-37, *36*

Ziles, Colonel, 48